Dayton Hartman has written a fin
tology, the doctrine of the last thir
an introduction to relevant biblica
held in the church over the centu....
ings against speculation and good encouragements to the u...,
church, since views of the last days have been terribly divisive over the
years. The book is written in an easy, conversational style, and it most
emphasizes what Scripture emphasizes, that through all the conflicts
of world history, Jesus wins.

John M. Frame
Retired J. D. Trimble Chair of
Systematic Theology and Philosophy,
Reformed Theological Seminary (Orlando)

Dayton Hartman is not only a gifted writer who brings the essentials of
theology from history to relevance in the present, he also does so in a
way that is clear, and clearly helpful. Jesus Wins is another fine example
of this as he helps all of us know with greater clarity the "reason for
the hope that is in us" as we await the return of our Lord Jesus. I hope
many people will read this book in these days.

Jason G. Duesing
Author of *Mere Hope: Life in an Age of Cynicism*,
Provost and Associate Professor of Historical Theology,
Midwestern Seminary

Hartman's book is an encouragement to the church that eschatology
is not a place for speculation but hope. Rather than be fearful about
the end, Hartman asks the church to unite around the essentials and
be about the work of the gospel with hope and assurance rather than
anxiety. This introduction to the hope of eschatology will be a welcome
resource for pastors and laity.

Russell Moore
President, The Ethics & Religious Liberty Commission
of the Southern Baptist Convention

Thinking about the end times can produce confusion, idle speculation, and fear. Dayton Hartman's *Jesus Wins* reminds us that this doesn't have to be the case. Instead, thinking biblically about eschatology brings clarity, confidence, and hope. This is because—as Hartman reminds us in biblical, theological, historical, and creedal ways—the simple truth is that Jesus wins. And that's good news! This book will edify, inform, and encourage every Christian, but especially those who want to understand more clearly what the Bible says about The End."

Matthew Y. Emerson
Associate Professor of Religion, Director of Master of Arts in
Christian Studies and Intercultural Studies Programs,
Oklahoma Baptist University

While views and interpretations of the end times vary (the author gives a very helpful explanation of the four primary views), the most important thing is how they all agree—Jesus will return and He wins. Dayton wisely uses the historical creeds (Apostles' Creed and Nicene Creed) and the development of Christian belief as a basis for his argument. For anyone who is overwhelmed or confused when thinking about how the world ends, I'd recommend this as a helpful resource and starting place.

Joby Martin
Lead Pastor at The Church of Eleven22

JESUS WINS

JESUS WINS

The

GOOD NEWS

of the

END TIMES

DAYTON HARTMAN

Foreword by Trevin Wax

LEXHAM PRESS

Jesus Wins: The Good News of the End Times

Copyright 2019 Dayton Hartman

Lexham Press, 1313 Commercial St., Bellingham, WA 98225
LexhamPress.com

All rights reserved. You may use brief quotations from this resource in presentations, articles, and books. For all other uses, please write Lexham Press for permission. Email us at permissions@lexhampress.com.

Unless otherwise noted, Scripture quotations are from the *ESV® Bible* (*The Holy Bible, English Standard Version®*), copyright 2001 by Crossway Bibles, a publishing ministry of Good News Publishers. Used by permission. All rights reserved.

Print ISBN 9781683591306
Digital ISBN 9781683591313

Lexham Editorial: Todd Hains, Abigail Stocker, and Danielle Thevenaz
Cover Design: Jim LePage
Typesetting: Abigail Stocker

For Redeemer Church.

Take heart! Jesus wins!

CONTENTS

ISAIAH 32:18

*My people will abide in
a peaceful habitation,
in secure dwellings, and
in quiet resting places.*

FOREWORD

The "end times" are a source of endless fascination for many Christians. Charts and graphs and timelines make their way into books and magazines and websites. Predictions come and go, prophets rise and fall, and the world just keeps on spinning.

I've had many a church member ask for a series through the book of "Revelations" (not knowing, I suspect, that the last book of the Bible is a *Revelation*—singular, and that Jesus is the One being revealed, not the specifics of a worldwide calamity reserved for the future). They're not wrong to wonder. After all, studying the end times, what we call "eschatology," is vitally important to the Christian life—not because it satisfies our curiosity but because it spurs us toward faithfulness. We labor in the Lord, knowing our work is not in vain, because the future is assured.

First Corinthians 15 is known to Bible readers as the "resurrection chapter." It's a portion of Scripture in which the apostle Paul lays out the reality of Jesus' resurrection from the dead, connects Jesus' resurrection in the past with Christians' resurrection in the future, and helps us see life and death in light of that resurrection power.

Curiously, after 57 verses of explaining the impact and significance of Jesus' resurrection, the apostle Paul gives a word of instruction: "Therefore, my dear brothers and sisters, be steadfast, immovable, always excelling in the Lord's work, because you know that your labor in the Lord is not in vain" (1 Cor 15:58 CSB). This chapter, focused so heavily on the end times, comes to a close with a powerful call to excellence in doing the Lord's work. Future glory will make sense of present suffering. God's work in the future gives meaning to our work in the present.

What is the future? Jesus wins! Properly understood, studying the end times is not a terrible distraction from our work but a terrific motivation for the tasks the Lord gives us. We do his work, trusting the One who holds the future (and the present).

This little book, *Jesus Wins*, serves as an accessible introduction to the topic of eschatology and the theology of what happens at the end of time. This book will help you navigate the various debates over what the Bible teaches. Dayton will help you understand this topic better, but he does so in a way that connects these truths to discipleship and to how we obey right now, in the present. In that sense, he is doing what Paul did in 1 Corinthians 15. He's explaining the future in order to empower our discipleship in the present. So, Christian, have hope! Be steadfast! Always excel in the Lord's work! Because of Jesus, your labor is not in vain.

Trevin Wax

Author of *This Is Our Time* and *Eschatological Discipleship*,

General Editor of The Gospel Project

REVELATION 22:12-13

Behold, I am coming soon, bringing my recompense with me, to repay each one for what he has done. I am the Alpha and the Omega, the first and the last, the beginning and the end.

CHAPTER 1

SCARED YET?

"No passion so effectively robs the mind of all its powers of acting and reasoning as fear."

—*Edmund Burke*

C *lang!* I hid my face in horror as the blade of a guillotine fell. Watching an off-camera beheading isn't exactly ideal pre-bedtime television for a child, but it was the 1980s—no bike helmets, searing hot metal playground slides, seatbelt-free station wagons. In short, a grim execution scene in a Christian movie—*A Thief in the Night*—was the least of my worries as a kid. Still, I was six years old, and I desperately wanted to escape the coming tribulation.

I was consumed with fear over the impending return of Christ.

As a child I was aware of the ever-increasing speculation about the end of the world and the return of Christ. Hal Lindsey's books were on my parents' bookshelves. Pat Robertson and Jack Van

Impe dominated Christian television. And every day someone new was proposing something new about the second coming—or rapture, depending on their theological commitments—whether Edgar Whisenant's *88 Reasons Why the Rapture Will Be in 1988* or Harold Camping's massive book *1994?*. The good news for Tim LaHaye and Jerry Jenkins was that both Whisenant and Camping were wrong. In 1995, their brand-new series, *Left Behind,* premiered with fanfare. The series has sold an estimated 65–75 million copies.

Harold Camping wasn't the only infamous leader involved in speculation and prophecy in the 1990s. The Christian world seemed to be consumed with thoughts of the end. The Y2K bug didn't help matters. Had Bill Gates, the founder of Microsoft, hardwired his computer systems to trigger the rise of a global

A THIEF IN THE NIGHT was a four-part movie series released between 1972 and 1983. These movies attempted to portray the presumed perils during the seven-year tribulation period central to dispensational eschatology.

HAROLD CAMPING (1921–2013) was the president of Family Radio. He tried to identify specific dates for the return of Christ and destruction of the world—twice: September 6, 1994, and May 21, 2011. After his prophecy failed to materialize, Camping issued a statement repenting of setting dates for Christ's return.

dictator and the collapse of every government? Surely the end is here! Even *The Los Angeles Times* covered the fever pitch of prophecy in 1999.[1]

The year 2000 arrived, and nothing happened. Bill Gates and the devil were not in cahoots to bring down the governments of the world. Maybe prophetic speculation would wane with the dawn of the new millennium. I mean, a self-professed evangelical was in the White House, so the end was still far off, right?

Everything changed on September 11, 2001. Once again, talk of the end dominated in American Christianity.

SPECULATION FADS

I used to manage a Christian bookstore—so I witnessed firsthand the fervor that came with any new book theorizing about the end of the world. I saw prophetic fads come and go. For a time, the *Left Behind* series was being answered by another fictional series from a partial-preterist perspective. The former host of the *Bible Answer Man* radio program, Hank Hanegraaff (1950–present), cowrote *The Last Disciple* series as a fictional narrative exploring the eschatological position from Hanegraaff's nonfiction book *The Apocalypse Code*.

After many publishing cycles of books filled with end-times speculation, two things remained consistent: First, speculators will always speculate. Second, when we prioritize prophetic speculation, we forget our mission and abandon the hope that Christian eschatology gives the church.[2] If you want to see Christians fight, bring up the end of the world.[3]

Once someone in our membership class asked me for our church's official position on the end times. I told him: "Our official position is that Jesus wins. We are free to disagree on the details of the timing and particulars of his victory, but he does win and that's what unites us in hope."

The man was frustrated. He told me that he loved our church, our approach to ministry,and our mission and vision, but he would have to find another church. That family left our fellowship more than two years ago—and to the best of my knowledge, they are still searching for a church to join. Later, the man told me how weary they were of the search. But they could not find a pastor with whom they agreed 100 percent on eschatological matters.

PARTIAL PRETERISM proposes that the majority of the prophecies described in Revelation were fulfilled in the events leading up to the destruction of the Jerusalem temple in AD 70. All that remains in the future are the final three chapters of Revelation.

HANK HANEGRAAFF (b. 1950) was the longtime host of the *Bible Answer Man* radio program until his conversion to Greek Orthodoxy in 2017. In response to *Left Behind*, Hanegraaff penned his novel *The Last Disciple*. This novel follows the partial-preterist understanding of prophecy wherein the events of the book of Revelation are largely fulfilled in the destruction of the temple complex in AD 70.

HAL LINDSEY (b. 1929) authored the book *The Late Great Planet Earth*. The New York Times dubbed it the best-selling nonfiction book of the 1970s. The book has sold tens of millions of copies. It continues to be influential among some Christians.

PAT ROBERTSON (b. 1930) is the longtime host of *The 700 Club* television program and chairman of the Christian Broadcasting Network. The 1988 presidential hopeful interprets current news in light of his particular brand of prophecy.

JACK VAN IMPE (b. 1931) is the host of a weekly prophetic news program titled *Jack Van Impe Presents*. In each episode, he tries to connect contemporary events to Bible prophecies.

Ironic, isn't it? By attempting to hold the line on what he believes is *the* biblical position on eschatology, he is eschewing the clear biblical mandate to be in community with other believers under the authority of biblically qualified elders. When we make secondary issues (like the timing and precise details of the end of days) primary issues, we make primary issues (such as church membership and fellowship with the saints) into secondary issues.

The position we have taken as a church is that believers are free to disagree about eschatological matters. Our congregation is made up of intelligent individuals who hold to historic premillennialism, dispensational premillennialism, amillennialism, and even some who lean postmillennial. Whether you are aware of it or not, your own beliefs are likely tied to one of these schools of interpretation. Good news! All of them are orthodox!

SPECULATION DEFERRED

How did I arrive at a "Jesus wins" eschatology? By reading church history. The Christian world—across time and place— is filled with rich theological traditions. The early church fathers navigated questions about persecution, church and state relationships, and authority, among others.[4] They weren't as concerned with wild-eyed theories as the average conspiracy-theory-loving American. And so it's little surprise that we have few early church texts on the end times. They had bigger problems. The church has generally allowed a variety of eschatological views (ruled by the Bible).

TIM LAHAYE (1926–2016) was a prolific writer and politically influential evangelical, best known for his *Left Behind* series. He worked closely with the leadership of the 1980s movement known as the Moral Majority.

While LaHaye provided the theological framework for the *Left Behind* series, seasoned novelist **JERRY JENKINS** (b. 1949) crafted LaHaye's theology into marketable works of fiction.

CLARIFYING TERMS: Many associate eschatology with a study of last things or the end times, but it more accurately describes Christian beliefs about the consummation of all things, the restoration of the created order, and eternity future.

I'm saddened by how often eschatological speculation derails the mission Jesus gave us: to make disciples. In fact, after more than a decade of ministry in the local church and teaching in seminaries and Christian colleges, I've yet to identify a single benefit from speculating about eschatology.

My original intention for this introduction was to list the dangers of speculation. But the list is neverending—and I've spent months on it! Every few days I think of another danger. Suffice it to just say: there is not a single benefit to eschatological speculation. None. Zero.

Speculation deemphasizes Jesus and leads to fear (which often leads to poor decision making). When we spend our days conjecturing about what may or may not happen before the second coming, we do so at the expense of the overwhelming hope that the second coming ought to give us.

By closely reading Scripture and church history, I've become convinced that a better way forward is to return to the eschatology of the Apostles' Creed. One of the oldest confessions of our faith, the creed simply states:

I believe in Jesus Christ, his only Son, our Lord.
He was conceived by the Holy Spirit
    and born of the virgin Mary.
He suffered under Pontius Pilate,
    was crucified, died, and was buried.
He descended to the dead.
On the third day he rose again.
He ascended into heaven
    and is seated at the right hand of the Father.
He will come to judge the living and the dead.

The eschatology of the creed does not foster fear or speculation—it calls for hope and anticipation, joy and confidence. (See chapter 5.) That's what Christian hope is all about, whether in the early church or today!

REVELATION 21:3

And I heard a loud voice from the throne saying, "Behold, the dwelling place of God is with man. He will dwell with them, and they will be his people, and God himself will be with them as their God."

CHAPTER 2

AWAITING THE END TIMES

*"What do we know? If I know what we know then I could
tell you what we know and if anyone else knows!"*

—*Jerry Fletcher, Conspiracy Theory*

For too many Christians, the purpose of our eschatological
belief is largely relegated to the realm of conspiracy theories,
discussion of scorched-earth fantasies, and fear of a coming
world dictator. Those are all the trappings of a Nic Cage summer
flopbuster. Yet, more than providing fodder for Hollywood,
Christian eschatology serves a specific purpose that ought to
consume every inch of our souls. The purpose of our eschatology shouldn't be voyeuristic fascination with destruction, but
rather hopeful anticipation of restoration. Russell Moore says

that our hope for restoration and redemption includes "table fellowship, community, culture, economics, agriculture and animal husbandry, art, architecture, worship—in short, life and that abundantly."[5] Christian eschatology ought to cause us to think about the future. But it has more to teach us about our lives here and now than whether Blackhawk helicopters are in Revelation.

SHOCKING NEWS

If you are asking "Are we living in the last days?" allow me to answer it for you: Yes! We are!

The author of Hebrews makes this clear:

> Long ago, at many times and in many ways, God spoke to our fathers by the prophets, but *in these last days* he has spoken to us by his Son, whom he appointed the heir of all things, through whom also he created the world. (Heb 1:1–2)

The incarnation marked the beginning of the end. The final age has begun. The last days are here and have been here for two thousand years!

Anglican theologian Gerald Bray has observed that this theme is central to the New Testament: "One of the most pervasive themes of the New Testament is that we are living in the last days and that will come to an end suddenly and without warning."[6] Dear Christian, you are living in the final days of history as we know it—just like Peter, Paul, and John.

CHANGING EXPECTATIONS

If we have been living in the last days for two thousand years, what is the purpose of Christian eschatological doctrine or belief? Simply put: Because Christ is present among his people—in an already-not-yet kind of way—we must live like it.

The story of humanity and its relationship to God began in the garden of Eden, and it ends with a return to Eden. The entire story of redemption is about getting us back to paradise. Our hope is not based on decoding the current news cycle; it's about living now as we once did and as we one day will live again. All of Christian eschatology is building toward a resolution inaugurated by Christ's life, death, resurrection, and ascension.

THE STORY OF THE BIBLE

The narrative of Scripture opens with creation, when God placed the first man and woman in Eden. Eden was not just humanity's place, and it was not exclusively God's place. It was the place on earth where God's place and our place converged. It's the place where God and people freely enjoyed one another.

While our interaction with God is different than what Adam and Eve experienced, not every aspect of life in Eden is foreign to us. There are a number of things in common—two specifically: work and relationship.

God made mankind to work in the garden (Gen 2:5, 15). We were created on purpose *for* a purpose. Some wrongly assume that work is the result of being in a fallen world, but work was God's original intention for mankind. Don't get the idea that in Eden humans were to lay around and be fed grapes by orangutans or have chinchillas awkwardly massaging our feet for hours on end. God made us for work. God created us to bring order to the world by expanding the place on earth where God and humans could meet (Eden). Work began as something good and enjoyable; difficulty and displeasure in work came after the fall (Gen 3). (As a result, Mike Rowe's *Dirty Jobs* could only occur in a world marred by sin.) We were made for work, and we enjoyed it.

God made humans to be relational. Shortly after creating Adam, God said that it is not good for man to be alone (Gen 2:18). After Adam named the animals, he realized that he had no equal to engage in relationship—as fun as his hypoallergenic golden doodle was. Thus, God creates Eve and brings her to Adam, and they are both overjoyed to have one another (Gen 2:22-25). God made us to be relational and communal beings.

We were designed to enjoy relationships and purposeful existence in his presence. You and I only experience our humanness to the fullest when we are living out our humanity in the presence of God. The garden of Eden was a convergence of God's place and humanity's place in such a way that we lived before the face of God.[7]

We were created to live in heaven on earth with our God. Then Adam killed the world. For a few pages humanity lived as we were created to live; everything falls apart in Genesis 3. Adam and Eve grasp for the throne of God by disobeying him and in so doing they bring sin and death into the world (Gen 3:1-7).

GOD'S PLACE AND MAN'S PLACE

HEAVEN

THE KINGDOM of GOD

GARDEN OF EDEN

GOD + MAN

EARTH

THE WORLD

For the first time Adam and Eve were afraid of God's presence in the garden (Gen 3:8) because the garden was no longer the place where God and humans could be together. They were now on enemy soil (Rom 1).

God's pronouncement of judgment in Genesis 3 makes clear that the world has now changed. Now work would be difficult and toilsome. Because of sin, Adam and Eve's relationship would be difficult. Death is now inevitable, and God's place no longer overlaps with humanity's place. Humans are expelled from the garden of Eden. We have been separated from God.

The remainder of the Bible is the story of God's work to get us back into his presence, back to the garden. Even the language that describes the temple system instituted by God is meant to point our hearts to the garden.[8]

Throughout the Bible, the temple and tabernacle descriptions nod to what we had in Eden. Through the temple system, God's place is accessible to humans but with extreme limitations. Because of sin, humans could only go so far toward the presence of God, hidden behind a veil in the temple.

Until God invaded our place in the person and work of his Son, Jesus! The incarnation of Jesus marks the beginning of the end of humanity's separation from God. Jesus appearing in human flesh put the world on notice that these days are the final days of separation (Heb 1:2). Restoration is coming. God's place and humanity's place will no longer be separated. That's why it is so significant that the veil in the temple was torn at Jesus' death on the cross (Matt 27:52). The veil that separated

EDEN & THE TEMPLE

SIMILARITY	EDEN	THE TEMPLE/TABERNACLE
Angels guard the entrance (from the east)	Gen 3:24	Exod 25:18–22
Lamp stand—with plant life molding—symbolized the Tree of Life	Gen 2:9; 3:22	Exod 25:31–35
Adam and the priests have the same job: to work and keep (abad), and to worship and obey (shamar)	Gen 2:15	Num 3:7–8; 8:26; 18:5–6
Gold and onyx are present	Gen 2:11–12	Exod 25:7–31
God is present	Gen 3:8	Lev 26:12; 2 Sam 7:6–7

the presence of God from the presence of humanity has been destroyed. The restoring of humanity's place with God himself has begun. Therefore, in Christ our relationship with God is restored already, but we are still awaiting physical restoration. That restoration is the point of our eschatological expectations.[9]

Still, we love to speculate—even the disciples were caught up in asking questions beyond what they needed to know. At the ascension of Jesus, the disciples are gathered and they have one final question to ask him: Is this the end? (Acts 1:6). They want to know if Jesus is going to "restore the kingdom to Israel" and bring about the messianic age of flourishing immediately. How does Jesus respond to their question? Well, forcefully: "It is not for you to know times or seasons that the Father has fixed by his own authority" (Acts 1:7). Jesus tells them, "Don't worry about it. I've won, I'm winning, and I will win." In light of that, Jesus commissions them to be his witnesses "to the end of the earth" (Acts 1:8). Jesus calls the disciples to stop worrying about the future and instead to trust and obey.

THE END IS THE BEGINNING

The restoration of all things, including humanity's place and God's place being reunited, is consummated in Revelation 21–22. In Revelation 21, the apostle John records the moment when heaven (pictured as a city) descends from the sky to formally and finally invade earth. God's place, heaven, is once again overlapping with humanity's place (earth).

EDEN & NEW JERUSALEM

SIMILARITY	EDEN	NEW JERUSALEM
The Tree of Life	Gen 2:9; 3:22	Rev 22:2
Rivers that give life	Gen 2:10	Rev 22:1–2
There is no death	Gen 3:22	Rev 21:4
Gold and onyx are present	Gen 2:11–12	Rev 21:18–20
God is present	Gen 3:8	Rev 21:4

Notice the similarities to the garden of Eden. In both places, God has provided a tree that ensures eternal life, rivers of life, and land littered with gold and onyx, and death is nowhere present. However, the key similarity is that God's presence and humans' presence are once again together. Because there is no longer sin and death, humans no longer need be terrified of God.

Christian eschatology points us to Eden restored. We get so caught up in the drama of Jesus returning on a warhorse (Rev 19) that we forget: he gets off his horse. When he dismounts, he reunites with his people (Rev 21). The same Jesus who comes on a warhorse against his enemies brings a home for his friends. Jesus gets us back home to heaven (God's place) on earth (our place): he gets us back to Eden. He gets us back to the place where we are truly human while wiping away the very things that make being human so hard: pain, heartache, regret (Rev 21:4). Does your heart ache? One day it won't! Is your body failing you? One day it won't. Does sadness mark your life? One day, only joy will define your existence. What you and I are awaiting is this moment that heaven returns to earth. According to Jesus, it will happen soon (Rev 22:7).[10]

HOW DOES THAT HELP ME NOW?

If the purpose of our eschatological hope is the restoration of all things, our own resurrection from the dead, and the reunion of humans and God, what does that mean for our here and now? We should live out the ethics of the coming kingdom in the present world.

The kingdom of Christ is already here through his church. Our churches are outposts or embassies of Christ's rule and reign. And yet we are still waiting for the return of the king with his kingdom in full.

In Matthew 24, Jesus begins a teaching passage commonly called the Olivet Discourse. There is a great deal of controversy regarding the signs he mentions in this text, along with much debate over the timing of these events. However, there is no debate over the implications of what he is teaching in light of Matthew 25: he wins. Evil will be punished and destroyed once and for all time.

In Matthew 25, Jesus turns his attention toward the final judgment. In this scene we are given a glimpse into the settled future in which victorious King Jesus issues final sentencing for all of humanity. Jesus places those under condemnation on his left and those under grace at his right hand. To those on the right, he begins listing off their good works. He says:

> "Come, you who are blessed by my Father, inherit the kingdom prepared for you from the foundation of the world. For I was hungry and you gave me food, I was thirsty and you gave me drink, I was a stranger and you welcomed me, I was naked and you clothed me, I was sick and you visited me, I was in prison and you came to me." Then the righteous will answer him, saying, "Lord, when did we see you hungry and feed you, or thirsty and give you drink? And when did we

see you a stranger and welcome you, or naked and
clothe you? And when did we see you sick or in prison
and visit you?" And the King will answer them, "Truly,
I say to you, as you did it to one of the least of these
my brothers, you did it to me." (Matt 25:34–40)

Jesus is not stating that his people are saved *by* their good
works but that they have been saved *for* good works. In Christ we
die to ourselves and are raised to true life with him. By his Spirit
this ultimate conversion is reflected in living the kingdom ethic.
Jesus describes the markers of an eternally minded believer.

In Christ we feed the hungry, because Jesus has given us
the bread of life. In Christ we meet the needs of the thirsty,
because Jesus has given us living water. In Christ we are kind
to the foreigner, because we were strangers in the land of sin
and death, and Jesus welcomed us into his kingdom of life. In
Christ we clothe others, because we were naked in our sin and
shame, and Jesus clothed us with his righteousness. In Christ
we care for the sick, because Jesus healed us from the disease
of sin. In Christ we love those in prison, regardless of what
they've done, because Jesus freed us from the bondage of sin
no matter what we've done. How do all these actions relate to
our salvation? Very simply: because Jesus has fed you the bread
of life, given you living water, welcomed you into his kingdom,
clothed you in righteousness, healed you from sin, and freed
you from bondage, you and I do the very things for others that
Jesus did for us.

For the believer, knowing that Jesus will come back and that he wins ought to drive us to live differently and distinctly from the world around us—to do for others what Jesus has done for us.[11] In so doing, we are reminding one another and giving the world a glimpse of what it will be like when heaven returns to earth. No one will be hungry, no one will be thirsty, no one will be naked, no one will be in bondage. This is the very thing Jesus did in his earthly ministry. Every time he healed someone, he showed us a world where sickness is no more. When he raised the dead, he was telling us that in his kingdom, death is defeated.[12]

LIVING CHRIST'S TRIUMPH

Jesus has won, is winning, and will win (all he does is win!). To live like this is the true means to recognize your present identity in Christ. In our baptism we are identified with the victory of Christ in his resurrection (Col 2:11–15). Jesus has canceled the debt we owed to the Father by nailing it to the cross.

> You, who were dead in your trespasses and the uncircumcision of your flesh, God made alive together with him, having forgiven us all our trespasses, by canceling the record of debt that stood against us with its legal demands. This he set aside, nailing it to the cross. He disarmed the rulers and authorities and put them to open shame, by triumphing over them in him. (Col 2:13–15)

And so we live now as if we are seated with Christ in the heavenly places—because we are. When Jesus returns, this reality will be visible before all. We live now as if the kingdom of heaven is on earth, because through God's people it is. And yet when Jesus returns, the kingdom will appear fully. Therefore, we must put to death our sin and put on the ethic of God's victorious kingdom people. Knowing that Jesus will return and will win changes not just your future but your present (Col 3:1–17).

We live knowing that we will one day get back to the garden when heaven comes to earth. Not only will death, sin, and Satan be defeated once and for all time, but we will again find our place and God's place overlapping. We will one day know what it is like to experience humanness to its fullest form when we do so in the presence of the Creator. Christian eschatology should be marked by awe-inducing adoration. Jesus is coming back, and he wins. So live like it.[13]

MATTHEW 24:36

But concerning that day and hour no one knows, not even the angels of heaven, nor the Son, but the Father only.

CHAPTER 3

VIEWS OF THE END TIMES

"Darkness must pass, a new day will come. And when the sun shines, it will shine out the clearer."

—Samwise Gamgee, *The Lord of the Rings*

When the movie *Independence Day* was released, I was a young teenager. My parents told me not to go see that movie. But a movie about an alien invasion? It was too much to resist! After watching nearly two hours of cities being destroyed by alien ships, I came away with three conclusions: First, my parents were right—I was too young for the movie. Second, Jeff Goldblum and Will Smith are the perfect action-movie duo. Third, I would never be able to forget the chorus to the R.E.M. song "It's the End of the World as We Know It (And I Feel Fine)."

That song expresses the human assumption that someday the world will end. As believers, we know it will end. And we know some of the *how* it will end—at least who wins in the end. We've done our best to mine the prophetic texts in Scripture to gain more and more detail that can be quantified and systematized to tell us how the world might end. It's comforting to know the details of something coming, even if it's ultimately beyond your control. To know what's ahead gives us some sense of security. So, for two thousand years, Christians have tried to piece together what the Bible says about the end.

A wide swath of orthodox interpretations are possible. This chapter explains the four broad eschatological categories: amillennialism, postmillennialism, historic premillennialism, and dispensationalism. Each of these views proposes a different take on three key aspects of the end of the world: the millennium, the binding of Satan, and the relationship between Israel and the church.

FIRE, JUDGMENT, AND THRONES

Revelation is the New Testament's mystery book. It's a difficult book in style and content. But this book provides the key text used in eschatological debates.[14] Revelation 20 describes a one-thousand-year reign of Christ, Satan's attempted rebellion on his way to judgment, and Christ's final judgment.

Satan is arrested. He's wrapped up in a chain and thrown into a bottomless pit to be held for a one-thousand-year period.

APOCALYPTIC LITERATURE is a genre about the disclosure or revelation of something that was mysterious or unknown. The book of Revelation is a key example of this genre. While many tend to think of "apocalyptic" as having to do with action movies involving major disasters, that's simply not the case. Instead, apocalyptic texts are filled with symbolic language and allegorical illustrations meant to point the reader to the truth being disclosed.

Those faithful to Christ—who died for his name and word and who refused to associate with the beast—are brought to life. They rule and reign with Christ for one thousand years. All others are dead.

At the end of this period, Satan is released for judgment, but he tries to organize a coup. He gathers allies from all over the globe for an assault on the kingdom of Christ; "their number is like the sand of the sea" (Rev 20:8). But as they march to destroy Christ's faithful, fire from heaven pours down on Satan's coconspirators and destroys them all. Satan and his minions are cast into the lake of fire.

After this battle, all the dead are judged: Are their names in the book of life? Death and Hades join Satan and his minions in the lake of fire.

How should Revelation 20 be interpreted? The answer to this question distinguishes the four categories. For example, a major sticking point between the views is what "one thousand years" means. It can literally mean one thousand years. But it can also indicate a very long time—even an eternity.[15]

AMILLENNIALISM

Amillennialism's name is a clear giveaway to its defining mark: "a-millennialism" literally means there is no literal, open, visible, one-thousand-year reign of Christ on earth. Instead, the reign of Christ is understood in a fundamentally different way.

Amillennialism does not have a specific antichrist as advocated in something like the *Left Behind* series. However, there may be a man of sin (2 Thess 2:1–12), who could fit some kind of antichrist definition or archetype in the modern understanding of the term.

The Reign of Christ: Amillennial thinkers note rightly that the one-thousand-year language describing the millennial period in Revelation 20 can be taken figuratively. So, the thousand-year period isn't a specific thousand-year cycle on an actual calendar. Instead, with his resurrection and ascension, Christ began his reign. He presently rules on earth (the millennial age) through his people. And he will return physically, at any moment, to usher in heaven on earth.

The Role of Satan: Satan's influence has been diminished because he has been bound by Christ. Satan himself is not presently exerting influence over the world.

Israel and the Church: There is not a stark contrast between Israel and the church. Rather, the church is spiritual Israel, because Christ is true Israel. This does not mean that the church has replaced Israel but instead that the church is the fulfillment of God's promises to Abraham that his offspring (Jesus) would bless all nations (people groups).

Key Passages: John 5:28–29; Romans 8:17–23; 2 Peter 3:3–14; 2 Thess 1:5–10.[16]

Notable Representatives: Augustine of Hippo, Martin Luther, John Calvin, Louis Berkhof, C. S. Lewis, R. C. Sproul.

No one has shaped the trajectory of the Western world more than **AUGUSTINE OF HIPPO** (354–430). A native of North Africa, Augustine's *The City of God* has shaped Western values for nearly two thousand years. Additionally, his works on theological subjects such as the doctrine of the Trinity (*De Trinitate*) have served as a bulwark for Christian orthodoxy.

MARTIN LUTHER (1483–1546) is most well-known for his Ninety-Five Theses, which fanned the early flames of the Protestant Reformation. However, some of Luther's greatest, if not lesser-known, contributions were his Small Catechism and his translation of the Bible into German.

Based in Geneva, **JOHN CALVIN** (1509–1564) was one of the most important Protestant Reformers. His seminal work, *Institutes of the Christian Religion*, which was meant to be read with his commentaries, is one of the most influential theological works of the Reformation.

POSTMILLENNIALISM

You have very likely never met a committed proponent of post-millennialism. That was not always the case. Early in American history, postmillennialism was, in some sense, an American eschatology. Now it's a theological peculiarity to hear someone speak of postmillennial ideas. In part, that's because postmillennialism is a difficult system to quantify. Not only is it a minority position, but postmillennial thinkers tend to disagree about the details. We will take a look at the broad points of agreement here.[17]

The Reign of Christ: Postmillennialists differ as to whether the reign of Christ is one thousand years or simply a long period of time. At its core, the distinctive of postmillennial thought is the ever-expanding progress of the gospel until the world becomes markedly Christian. Then, Christ returns. The millennial age is ushered in by the unrelenting advance of the gospel.

The Role of Satan: There is no definitive position on the role of Satan within postmillennial thought. Some postmillennial theologians argue that Satan was bound by Jesus (similar to amillennialism), while others would argue it remains a future event (in agreement with premillenialism).

Israel and the Church: The postmillennial position agrees with amillennialism: the church is the fulfillment of Israel. The church is spiritual Israel.

Key Passages: Psalm 2; Isaiah 2:2–4; Matthew 13, 28; John 12.

Notable Representatives: Jonathan Edwards, B. B. Warfield, Greg Bahnsen, Loraine Boettner, Kenneth Gentry, Peter Leithart.

PREMILLENNIALISM

Premillennialism is often assumed to be the default view of Christians in America. This is understandable—it is presently the most common view of eschatology held by American evangelicals. While evangelicals are most familiar with the primary framework of premillennial thought, many are unaware that premillennialism has two major divisions: historic premillennialism (the traditional form, often called simply "premillennialism") and dispensational premillennialism (usually called "dispensationalism").[18]

HISTORIC PREMILLENNIALISM

The Reign of Christ: Christ will return physically and visibly in order to usher in the millennial reign—but historic premillennialists disagree whether the reign of Christ will be a literal thousand years or just a long period of time.

The Role of Satan: Satan is currently at work in the world, influencing affairs and deceiving the nations. At the return of Christ, Satan will be bound for the duration of the millennial age.

Israel and the Church: Historic premillennialism proposes that the church is the spiritual fulfillment of Israel in a manner that is very similar to amillennialism and postmillennialism.

Key Passages: This position shares many of the same key passages as amillennialism and postmillennialism. The distinction between the systems has to do with interpretation. Premillennialism places a heavier emphasis on rigidly literal interpretations of key passages than either amillennialism or postmillennialism does.

Notable Representatives: Irenaeus, Wayne Grudem, Robert Gundry, Ben Witherington III, Craig Blomberg.

DISPENSATIONALISM

The Reign of Christ: For the majority of dispensationalists, the millennial reign of Christ will begin after his return, at the end of a distinct seven-year period known as the tribulation. The millennial reign of Christ begins at the third coming of Christ. Dispensationalists propose a secret rapture concept in which Christ returns (prior to or midway through the tribulation period) to remove the church from the earth.

The Role of Satan: Like historic premillennialism, dispensationalism argues that Satan is actively at work to resist the church and to undermine God's people. He will be bound for the duration of the millennium and only released for a final confrontation following his one-thousand-year captivity.

The **SECRET RAPTURE** is a dispensationalist doctrine that proposes that the second coming takes place in two stages: First, Christ returns secretly, in the clouds, to snatch from earth all those who profess saving faith in Christ. Second, at a later date Christ will physically return, with those whom he raptured from the earth, to establish his earthly kingdom.

Israel and the Church: Dispensationalism envisions the church and Israel as two distinct entities in God's redemptive plan. God's primary plan is for the redemption of Israel. His secondary plan, which is often described as "parenthetical," is for the salvation of the gentiles through the church.

Key Passages: While dispensationalism also shares premillennialism's more literal approach to the key passages, dispensationalism holds Daniel 9 (on the seventy weeks) as a key passage for interpreting the arc of history. Additionally, classic dispensationalism proposes that the content of the Bible is divided along seven dispensations (or eras). While different schools of dispensationalism categorize these eras differently, one common structure is innocence, conscience, human government, promise, law, grace, and the millennium. Key passages are interpreted through this dispensational framework.

Notable Representatives: Lewis S. Chafer, John Walvoord, Charles Ryrie, Hal Lindsey, John MacArthur.

SUMMARY OF THE VIEWS

There's actually quite a bit of agreement among the various eschatological views. Regarding the reign of Christ: amillennialists (and some postmillennialists) understand the number one thousand in Revelation as a symbol and the character of Christ's reign as spiritual; premillennialists (and some postmillennialists) take the number one thousand literally and understand the character of Christ's reign to be visible. Everyone agrees

In classic dispensationalism, **THE SEVENTY WEEKS** of Daniel 9 are viewed as a timeline for world events. Each of the weeks represents a seven-year period of time. The first sixty-nine weeks have already occured; we are waiting for the seventieth week. The seventieth week marks the start of the seven-year tribulation period that is distinctive of dispensationalism.

PROGRESSIVE DISPENSATIONALISM differs from classical dispensationalism in its strong adherence to the "already but not yet" approach to understanding the kingdom of Christ on earth. Additionally, this new system does not hold as stark of a division between the church and Israel as proponents of classical dispensationalism do.

that Satan is bound during the millennium. Postmillennialists stick out a bit here, since they disagree over what constitutes the beginning of the millennium. Amillennialists, historic premillennialists, and postmillennialists agree that the church is the fulfillment of Israel. Dispensationalists sharply distinguish Israel and the church.

Complicating any effort to distinguish between each of these views is the fact that they share key passages but interpret them differently. History helps clarify areas of agreement and points of departure.

THE HISTORY OF THE END TIMES

Shortly after the deaths of the apostles, basic interpretations of the millennium appeared in early Christian histories and letters.[19] One of the oldest traditions comes from a man named Papias. Not much is known about Papias; we know that he knew the apostle John personally, and it's usually assumed that he was born around AD 70 and died in the 120s. Eusebius (c. 260–340), one of the first church historians, records that Papias taught that Jesus will physically rule and reign on earth for one thousand years.[20] Eusebius doesn't include Papias' argument. He just reports it and then promptly blasts it: "I suppose he got these ideas through a misunderstanding of the apostolic accounts."[21]

Papias and Eusebius approached the millennium with different foundational theological assumptions. These assumptions were so different that Eusebius could only explain Papias' view as a misunderstanding. If he had lived in the same era, Papias may have very well said the same of Eusebius' view.

Papias seems to have assumed a strictly plain, literal meaning of Revelation 20: Christ will return and reign from an earthly throne for a set period of one thousand years. But the circumstances of his contemporaries, the early Christians, may have also influenced his view. Christians were marginalized, slaughtered, and largely relegated to positions of poverty. The millennium is to be a time of comfort and peace. So some Christians saw it as a time when Christians would rule in luxury and wealth.

Eusebius wasn't the only one baffled by this understanding of the millennium; Origen and Augustine, among others, also took a different approach. They read Revelation 20, knowing that God's ways are wholly unlike ours. "My thoughts are not your thoughts, neither are your ways my ways" (Isa 55:8). For Eusebius, Origen, and Augustine, what could be more unfitting than a literal one-thousand-year reign of excess and earthly power?

In that time period, too, circumstances may have influenced their views more than we initially realize. The tensions between the church and the government (and society at large) had diminished. In an age of increasingly positive relations between the church and the state, the emphasis of amillennialism seemed to be confirmed. It made sense to an increasing number of Christians that the church existed in the millennial age: the rule of Christ brought peace between the church and the institution that once oppressed her.

ORIGEN (d. 254) was one of the most controversial and influential theologians in the early church. Known for his love of allegorical (spiritual) interpretation, Origen penned hundreds of works in theology, linguistics, and commentary resources.

JUSTIN MARTYR (c. 100–165) was one of the first Christian philosophers. Justin used the apostle John's *logos* language to explain the deity of Jesus to his audience. He was also one of the first to publicly defend the Christian right to worship.

The **ANABAPTISTS** were part of the Radical Reformation that sought overthrow of the Roman Catholic Church and subsequent restoration of the true church—on occasion even through violent means. While Luther and his followers sought true Reformation of the Roman Church, Radical Reformers thought that mere reformation did not go far enough.

Justin Martyr points out that the early church—before Eusebius apparently—tolerated both premillennialism and amillennialism.[22] But this early church diversity converged into an amillennial consensus.[23]

The Reformers, like Martin Luther and John Calvin, were also amillennial, following in Augustine's footsteps. They found the premillennialism of some of the Radical Reformers repulsive, as if these folks sought to understand God's categories through human categories. Sort of like Eusebius' estimation of Papias.

Amillennialism remained the only show in town until the Puritans introduced some variety. (Around the same time, premillennialism was revived by Pietists.) Some Puritans envisioned the New World as a guiding light to the nations.[24] And so theologians like John Owen popularized the hopeful eschatology of postmillennialism. Jonathan Edwards—who didn't speak publicly about his millennial speculation—reimagined America as a bastion of gospel hope: a people that would lead the nations into the millennial age and beyond.[25]

The Great Awakening seemed to confirm this special work that God intended to take place in the New World. And many colonists saw the American Revolution as a clean break from the Old World. Might this new beginning commence the millennial reign of Christ?[26] Postmillennialism grew in popularity after the American victory over the British.

But postmillennialism's advance came to a grinding halt around the time of the American Civil War. The conflict was a serious blow to the hope that this nation was the impetus for Christ's millennial reign. As the nineteenth century turned into the twentieth century, the future of the world was uncertain. Optimism faded as fear and pessimism reigned. Americans grappled with the devastation left by the Civil War, the terrors of

JOHN OWEN (1616–1683) was a prolific author whose most famous works are *The Death of Death in the Death of Christ* and *The Mortification of Sin*. His most famous quote comes from *The Mortification of Sin*: "Be killing sin or it will be killing you."

THE GREAT AWAKENING was a time of revival that began to take shape in 1734. It's often associated with the preaching ministry of Jonathan Edwards (1703–1758), considered the most influential American theologian. By 1735, some twenty-five communities had reported outbreaks of religious enthusiasm resulting from what Edwards called the "frontier revival."

World War I, the Great Depression, and the difficulties of modernization. People wanted an explanation for what was happening, and American postmillennialism wasn't doing the trick. Enter the new kid on the block: dispensationalism. With its eye always on the current news cycle, dispensationalism supplied a mechanism for explaining the world.[27]

John Nelson Darby, a British minister, is the man most responsible for this new breed of premillennialism. Convinced that the Protestant denominations were in ruins, Darby joined a burgeoning movement, based in Dublin, known as the Plymouth Brethren. Among this separatist group, Darby sought to explain the world around him through his specific reimagining of historic premillennialism. As a pastor, Darby spread his view of the end times through prophecy conferences.

However, the most efficient vehicle to spread Darby's eschatology was a study Bible. C. I. Scofield's study Bible—which largely followed Darby's prophetic outline—spread dispensational thinking throughout America.

Dispensationalism found a welcoming partner in Christian Fundamentalism. With increasing threats from Marxist thought, secularism, Darwinian evolution, and the growth of Modernism, those holding to the fundamentals of the Christian faith began to pull out of denominational coalitions (including the schools and seminaries associated with those denominations).

Disenchanted, Fundamentalists founded their own colleges and seminaries—often with a distinctly dispensational approach. Dallas Theological Seminary, Grace Theological

JOHN NELSON DARBY (1800–1882) had a brief career as a lawyer before becoming a priest for the Church of Ireland. During his ministry he become disillusioned with the denominational church. He also believed that the telegraph was the harbinger of Armageddon.

The **PLYMOUTH BRETHREN** began in 1829 in southern England as a dissident movement rebelling against the Anglican Church.

C. I. SCOFIELD (1843–1921) was a former soldier and district attorney who became an influential thinker in the burgeoning dispensational movement.

Seminary, and Moody Bible Institute are among the most influential of these schools. Generations of pastors were (and are!) trained in these institutions.

To their credit, these schools remained committed to the central tenants of Christian orthodoxy at a time when many seminaries were debating the authority of the Bible. Conservative Christians seeking theological education often sought training in these institutions, which furthered the spread of dispensationalism.

Decades after the birth of these institutions (and others), classical dispensationalism is waning. There are at least two reasons for this. First, classic dispensationalism's explanatory power has diminished: decades after the rebirth of Israel as a nation, the expected (final?) countdown to Christ is still on pause, and the Cold War, regularly promoted as evidence for the growing power of the antichrist, has ended. Second, there has been a revival of historical theology in seminaries and local churches, exposing students and congregants to systems they may have otherwise never known.

A COMMON HOPE

The great tradition of the church puts a different emphasis on eschatology than many modern Christians do. Early church historian Ronald Heine says this well: "No one ever seems to

THE FUNDAMENTALS was a series of pamphlets published between 1910 and 1915 (edited by A. C. Dixon and R. A. Torrey). These short treatments of Bible doctrine were intended to reaffirm the basics of the Christian faith. This should not be confused with the contemporary usage of the term "Fundamentalist," which has come to be used as a pejorative toward those in legalistic denominations.

MODERNISM is a system of thought that sought to accommodate Christianity to contemporary culture and the most current science. Modernists rejected the authority claims of the Bible, along with doctrines such as special creation and the virgin birth.

have been pronounced heretical solely on the basis of his or her understanding of Revelation 20. We should learn from that toleration of diverse views in the early church and let that example guide us in our thinking about the millennial question."[28]

It's tempting to identify the oldest Christian position on the end times as the correct position. But we need to examine a position's faithfulness to the Bible, not how old it is or how many people hold it. If the oldest Christian stance is the right one on every issue, we're in trouble! During the time between Christ's crucifixion and resurrection, all of the disciples denied the resurrection of the dead. And surely the majority doesn't determine right doctrine—otherwise, the Jerusalem Council (Acts 15) would have decreed that all gentiles must be circumcised and follow the letter of the Torah.

Yes, we can rank the four approaches to eschatology according to their popularity throughout the church's life.[29] We can also emphasize their areas of disagreement. Despite differences on the millennial age, the events leading up to the return of Christ, and the relationship between Israel and the church, these eschatologies agree about more than they disagree. None of these deny the basic eschatology of the Apostles' Creed: "He will come to judge the living and the dead."

We share one central hope in Jesus' victory. We should discuss which system(s) most faithfully and consistently interpret the Bible, but we must do so knowing that our hope is a shared hope. Our hero is the same. Jesus returns, and Jesus wins.

ZECHARIAH 14:9

*And the LORD will be
king over all the earth. On
that day the LORD will be
one and his name one.*

CHAPTER 4

WHAT THE CREEDS SAY ABOUT THE END TIMES

"You shall not cause division, but shall make peace between those who quarrel."

—*The Didache*

If you grew up in a church, you know that Christians can argue over incredibly dumb things. Sure, Jesus told us the world will know us by our love for one another, but this is serious—new carpet in the sanctuary! It's amazing! Why *wouldn't* you want it?

Now, my own tradition? Well, Southern Baptists' favorite pastime is arguing. We value the autonomy of local churches and we believe in congregational church government. This can result in some wild and wacky—or just mean and angry—debates over silly issues. Thankfully, most denomination-wide skirmishes have been justified. Our battle over the authority of the Bible was worth "going to the mat." But there have been other, less-justified struggles, too: whether Baptists officially embrace Calvinism over Arminianism, how often we should observe the Lord's Supper, and the "worship wars" of the 1990s (fine, Chris Tomlin—you win).

Yet, as our culture veers toward antipathy to Christian faith, perhaps we—as Christians—should fight less and agree more. There should be increasing solidarity within traditions and across traditions.

The more splintered we are over secondary doctrinal issues, the less effective we are in the mission that Jesus gave us. Christian cooperation in gospel expansion must be predicated

CALVINISM is a Reformed theological system associated with the teachings of John Calvin. It's often summarized with the acronym TULIP (total depravity, unconditional election, limited atonement, irresistible grace, and preservation of the saints). Calvinism emphasizes the sovereignty of God in salvation.

ARMINIANISM is based upon the teachings of Jacob Arminius (1559–1609) that emphasized the free will of human beings. Arminius formulated his theology as an intentional response to the teachings of the Reformation.

upon a return to creedal Christianity: we define the essentials upon which all Christians agree by the early ecumenical creeds.

THE CREEDS' ESCHATOLOGY

Simply put, the creeds are memorable, faithful summaries of what the Bible teaches and what Christians have always believed. For children of the Reformation, the early creeds faithfully present accurate summaries of biblical orthodoxy that reflect *sola Scriptura*. Creeds can be the rallying point for Christian cooperation because they act as orthodox guardrails for theologians and pastors.

I like to think of the relationship between Scripture and creeds as a highway. Scripture is our starting point. It defines the direction and content of biblical orthodoxy. Our journey in biblical orthodoxy must take place within the lanes provided by Scripture. Within those lanes, Christians can disagree and remain on the safe road of biblical orthodoxy. Think of the lanes as different Christian traditions—Reformed, Wesleyan, or charismatic, for example.[30] The guardrails of the creeds protect those traveling along the highway of biblical orthodoxy. While allowing for diversity on nonessential issues, the creeds prevent us from veering away from biblical orthodoxy. Because the safeguards exist, the only way to leave the safe road of orthodoxy is to do a great deal of damage.[31]

In light of this, two creeds (in particular) should serve as the basis for Christian cooperation. (We'll look more at a third creed, the Athanasian Creed, in an appendix later in the book.) Millions of Christians around the globe confess these truths daily. First, the Apostles' Creed. The Apostles' Creed bubbled up from the beliefs of everyday Christians. Australian theologian Ben Myers describes this creed as a "grassroots confession of faith."[32] Although it bears the name "the Apostles' Creed," this text did not originate with the apostles themselves but rather with the sacramental and catechetical practices of those passing on the teaching of the apostles.[33] In reading through the creed, you will note that these are the beliefs of all Christians for all time. There is nothing innovative here. Instead, these are sturdy, ancient truths that have stood the test of time and challenges from heresy.

> I believe in God, the Father almighty,
> creator of heaven and earth.
>
> I believe in Jesus Christ, his only Son, our Lord.
> He was conceived by the Holy Spirit
>   and born of the Virgin Mary.
> He suffered under Pontius Pilate,
>   was crucified, died and was buried.
> He descended to the dead.
> On the third day he rose again.
> He ascended into heaven,
>   and is seated at the right hand of the Father.
> *He will come to judge the living and the dead.*

I believe in the Holy Spirit,
the holy Christian church,
the communion of saints,
the forgiveness of sins,
the resurrection of the body,
and the life everlasting. Amen.

Notice the italicized portions of the creed: these phrases speak to Christian eschatology. There are no charts, no speculation, just confidence that Jesus gives us true life and mends what's broken—both now and, ultimately, in his return. Beyond this confidence, there is unwavering hope that when Jesus wins, we will rise to resurrected life.

Second, the Nicene Creed. In contrast to the Apostles' Creed, the Nicene Creed is the direct result of deliberations in an official council filled with bishops and other folks with important-sounding titles. In the years prior to the Council of Nicaea (AD 325), the teachings of a man named Arius gained notoriety. Arius' central claim was that Jesus is not the eternal Son of God but rather a creation of the eternal God. The council was convened to reaffirm the biblical teaching of the deity and eternality of Christ.[34] And so they wrote:

I believe in one God,
the Father, the Almighty,
maker of heaven and earth,
of all that is, seen and unseen.

I believe in one Lord, Jesus Christ,
the only Son of God,
eternally begotten of the Father,
God from God, Light from Light,
true God from true God,
begotten, not made,
of one Being with the Father.
Through him all things were made.
For us and for our salvation
    he came down from heaven:
by the power of the Holy Spirit
    he became incarnate from the Virgin Mary,
    and was made man.
For our sake he was crucified under Pontius Pilate;
    he suffered death and was buried.
    On the third day he rose again
        in accordance with the Scriptures;
    he ascended into heaven
        and is seated at the right hand of the Father.
He will come again in glory to judge the living and the
    dead,
    and his kingdom will have no end.

I believe in the Holy Spirit, the Lord, the giver of life,
who proceeds from the Father and the Son.
With the Father and the Son he is worshiped and
    glorified.

He has spoken through the prophets.
I believe in one holy Christian and apostolic church.
I acknowledge one baptism for the forgiveness of sins.
I look for the resurrection of the dead,
   and the life of the world to come. Amen.

Looking again at the italicized portions of the creed, there is nothing present but confident hope in the return and victory of Christ. The Nicene Creed outlines the same Christian essentials as the Apostles' Creed—with a focused response to Arianism. The Nicene Creed agrees with the Apostles' Creed. When it comes to eschatology, Christians are united in one hope.

We need to return to the creeds' eschatology. That's not to say that our eschatological exploration should never exceed the content of the creeds. No! Instead, the particulars of our eschatological convictions ought never contradict nor supersede the uniting Christian hope of Christ's assured return and victory.[35]

ARIANISM teaches that Jesus was created, rather than the historic Christian belief that Jesus is the eternal Son of God. It's named after an Egyptian pastor Arius (250–336). He was also one of the first pop artists; he publicized his teaching through rhyming chants and gained widespread popularity. The spread of Aruis' teaching led, in part, to the Council of Nicaea.

THE HOPELESSNESS OF
CULTURAL ESCHATOLOGY

American Christians live in difficult times culturally and politically. We seem to have lost the culture war. And politically we're wandering in the wilderness. If your hope is tied to political or cultural renewal as the evidence of Christ's work in the world, then you will eventually find yourself in despair. But eschatology ought to bring hope!

So, why do many feel so hopeless? Here are two observations:

1. *The news cycle is always pessimistic.* Controversy and scandal drive the news of our day. If it's not shocking or terrifying, we tend not to pay attention. Therefore, the news media knows it must continue to publish provocative and even fear-inducing content in order to drive subscriptions and consumption. Our theology is far more influenced by our cultural context than we realize. It is cliché but true: theology is not formed in a vacuum. This cloud of despair over our culture drives us toward hopelessness in our theology.

2. *We have neglected the simple eschatological hope that Jesus will return, and when he does, he wins.* We tend to approach eschatology either as an impulse toward intense, conspiracy-theory-esque speculation or as a subject that should be ignored to avoid

debates. Jesus must be at the center of our eschatology, or our best-concocted theories will fail to reflect the truth of God's plans.

So, what is the answer to our predicament? Should we turn off the news? Maybe! The news cycle will always be a drag on one's soul. Nevertheless, while ignorance may be bliss, it is still ignorance. What would be most beneficial to us is to interpret the news cycle in light of what we know to be true: no matter how difficult the days become, Jesus is coming soon, and Jesus wins.

THE HOPE OF THE CREEDS' ESCHATOLOGY

Practically, how do we interpret the news in light of Jesus' second coming?

Um, maybe not by diving into controversies about amillennialism, postmillennialism, and premillennialism?

The answer to our angst is much simpler. To have hope for the future, we need to look back.

The earliest Christians were the target of a hostile, nearly global empire. The first believers were the subject of vicious accusations from a world that did not understand them. They were wrongly accused of incest, cannibalism, and child sacrifice, just to name a few. Yet they held strongly to an undeniable hope. This hope was not because they had the details and dates of eschatology figured out. If we look to the early church, the first believers were united in the hope-inducing conviction that Jesus is returning—soon—and that when he does, he will be the victor. While this didn't save them from the pain and suffering of this world, it did give them the endurance to trust Christ to the end.

They endured because they believed in the sovereignty of God. Our God is the Creator who rules over time and the affairs of humankind. When peace rules in our nation or the nations, our God reigns. When genocidal maniacs wipe out villages, our God still reigns—storing up judgment against those who commit injustice.

The Psalms provide examples of holding our pain, anger, and frustration before God and others. Consider Psalm 13: "How long, O LORD? Will you forget me forever? How long will you hide your face from me? How long must I take counsel in my soul and have sorrow in my heart all the day? How long shall my enemy be exalted over me?" (vv. 1–2). The apparent victory of evil over good and the presence of tragedy instead of peace break our hearts. But confession and prayer move us from despair to trust. The psalmist cries out in pain and abandonment. And in his cries he is reminded of God's steadfast love. Confidence in Christ's victory doesn't mean we won't experience loss, fear, and suffering. But he will bring justice at his second coming, and the One we cry out to in our despair hears us and answers us: "I have trusted in your steadfast love; my heart shall rejoice in your salvation" (v. 5). No matter the circumstances of national and global tragedies and triumphs, our God is supreme, and the time until his return grows shorter each day.

Resist the urge to despair at the state of affairs in our nation and our world by joining the early church in simply and confidently confessing: Jesus is coming soon, and Jesus wins. No matter how dark the days grow, confidence in the final and ultimate victory of Jesus ought to bring hope to even the most pessimistic of people. Regardless of where we land on the spectrum of eschatological interpretations, we agree on far more than we disagree.

REVELATION 21:4

He will wipe away every tear from their eyes, and death shall be no more, neither shall there be mourning, nor crying, nor pain anymore, for the former things have passed away.

CHAPTER 5

GOOD NEWS! IT'S THE END

"In essentials unity, in nonessentials liberty, in all things charity."

—*Traditionally attributed to Augustine of Hippo*

Believers need to adopt a specific school of eschatology as the natural end and hope of their theology. Our theology matters! What we believe about the future will drive our engagement with or our withdrawal from culture. This is no small matter.

Yet we ought to once again look to the creeds as a template for defining orthodoxy, especially in a theological category as divisive as eschatology. We ought to hold to our denominational distinctives with great conviction. We can and should discuss and debate—in a healthy, respectful manner—the difference between our different denominations. Nevertheless, as long as we all remain within the guardrails of our faith (the creeds), we must see one another as brothers and sisters in Christ.

UNITY WITH OTHERS

Martyn Lloyd-Jones was an opinionated man if there ever was one. He believed that pastors should preach in robes—maybe he thought robes conveyed the seriousness of the pastoral office or, more likely, because he hated happiness and comfort. However, his opinions on eschatology were pretty solid: he argued that one's eschatology should never be used as a test for orthodoxy so long as it falls within the historically orthodox positions of our faith. We must define points of agreement that represent the far reaches of orthodoxy and then be willing to admit that what lies beyond those shores of sure things are simply speculative things.[36]

I agree: "Jesus wins" is the Christian approach to eschatological unity.

Together for the Gospel exemplifies this well. This conference is a feast for lovers of expositional preaching (as well as lovers of Louisville "beer cheese"). The lineup of speakers is always incredibly diverse. There's Matt Chandler's high-speed, culturally engaged preaching and John MacArthur's Puritan-esque parsing-of-every-word preaching. There are Baptists and Presbyterians united together (with God, all things are possible). And there are dispensationalists, historic premillennialists, amillennialists, and those who are somewhere in-between. The conference focuses on what unites us: the good news of the

MARTYN LLOYD-JONES (1899–1981) spent three decades serving as a pastor for Westminster Chapel and the eventual president of Inter-Varsity Fellowship of Evangelical Unions (the antecedent to InterVarsity Christian Fellowship in the United States). A strong proponent of expository preaching, Lloyd-Jones influenced a generation of pastors to take seriously the Scriptures and to preach clearly on theological matters.

gospel. Together for the Gospel exists because people are willing to hold their eschatological positions as secondary convictions.

For those who love eschatology and the gospel, let me make this clear: when we make secondary matters as important as primary matters, we diminish the importance of primary matters rather than elevating the importance of secondary issues.

There is much to parse on the nature of the atonement, the interpersonal relationships of the Persons of the Godhead, the elective decrees of God, and even how the consummation of all things will occur. Yet, the guardrail of our eschatology is the creedal hope, profession, and proclamation that Jesus returns and wins.

VICTORY IN CHRIST

The cross, resurrection, and ascension of Christ parade his victory over death, hell, and our enemy the devil. With Athanasius, we look back on the finished work of Christ and say:

As when a tyrant has been defeated by a legitimate king and bound hand and foot, all those that then pass by mock him, hitting and reviling him, no longer fearing his fury and barbarity because of the victorious king; in this way death also having been conquered and placarded by the Savior on the cross, and bound hand and foot, all those in Christ who pass by trample on [death], and witnessing to Christ they mock death, jeering at him, and saying what was written above, "O death, where is your victory? O hell, where your sting?"[37]

Dear Christian, we know what our future holds, because our king walked out of the grave. And he will return in the clouds.

How do we lay claim to this hope in everyday life? First, identify and repent of the ways in which you have allowed speculation to distract you from the hero of our eschatology: Jesus. Second, regardless of your eschatological conviction, study other positions to better understand what believers from other traditions believed. Third, reclaim the purpose of our eschatology: to give us hope for today and tomorrow.

> *Therefore, let us proclaim the mystery of our faith:*
> *Christ has died.*
> *Christ is risen.*
> *Christ will come again.*[38]

MICAH 4:3

He shall judge between
*   many peoples,*
*   and shall decide disputes for*
*   strong nations far away;*
and they shall beat their
*   swords into plowshares,*
*   and their spears into*
*   pruning hooks;*
nation shall not lift up
*   sword against nation,*
*   neither shall they learn*
*   war anymore.*

APPENDIX 1

SUGGESTED READING

We need to return to creedal eschatology for the sake of gospel unity—and we will benefit from learning the specifics of our eschatological anticipation. Here are some books I've found to be very helpful in my own journey. These titles represent a variety of eschatological views because we all benefit from having our own presuppositions challenged.

GENERAL ESCHATOLOGY

Three Views on the Millennium and Beyond, edited by Darrell L. Bock

The Meaning of the Millennium: Four Views, edited by Robert G. Clouse

The Bible and the Future by Anthony A. Hoekema

These Last Days: A Christian History edited by Richard D. Phillips and Gabriel N. E. Fluhrer

BIBLICAL ESCHATOLOGY

From Eden to the New Jerusalem: An Introduction to Biblical Theology by T. Desmond Alexander

Making All Things New: Inaugurated Eschatology for the Life of the Church by Benjamin L. Gladd and Matthew S. Harmon

The Promise of the Future by Cornelis P. Venema

AMILLENNIALISM

A Case for Amillennialism: Understanding the End Times by Kim Riddlebarger

The Last Days according to Jesus: When Did Jesus Say He Would Return? by R. C. Sproul

Kingdom Come: The Amillennial Alternative by Sam Storms

POSTMILLENNIALISM

Postmillennialism: An Eschatology of Hope by Keith A. Mathison

He Shall Have Dominion: A Postmillennial Eschatology by Kenneth L. Gentry, Jr.

The Millennium by Loraine Boettner

HISTORIC PREMILLENNIALISM

A Case for Historic Premillennialism: An Alternative to "Left Behind" Eschatology, edited by Craig L. Blomberg and Sung Wook Chung

The Last Things: An Eschatology for Laymen by George Eldon Ladd

Daniel and the Latter Days by Robert Duncan Culver

DISPENSATIONALISM

Dispensationalism by Charles Ryrie

Things to Come: A Study in Biblical Eschatology by J. Dwight
      Pentecost

*The Case for Progressive Dispensationalism: The Interface between
      Dispensational and Non-Dispensational Theology* by Robert
      L. Saucy

HISTORICAL THEOLOGY

The Last Days Are Here Again: A History of the End Times by
      Richard Kyle

The Hope of the Early Church: A Handbook of Patristic Eschatology
      by Brian E. Daley

*Regnum Caelorum: Patterns of Millennial Thought in Early
      Christianity* by Charles E. Hill

The Puritan Hope: Revival and the Interpretation of Prophecy by
      Iain H. Murray

HEAVEN AND HELL

Heaven by Randy Alcorn

Life Everlasting: The Unfolding Story of Heaven by Dan C. Barber
      and Robert A. Peterson

*Hell Under Fire: Modern Scholarship Reinvents Eternal
      Punishment*, edited by Christopher W. Morgan and Robert
      A. Peterson

REVELATION 21:5

And he who was seated on the throne said, "Behold, I am making all things new." Also he said, "Write this down, for these words are trustworthy and true."

THE ATHANASIAN CREED

In chapter 4, I noted the eschatological assertions of three of the most influential creeds in the history of the church. I quoted two of those creeds (the Nicene and Apostles' Creeds) in full. Here, I share the third creed—the Athanasian Creed. Despite this creed's title, Athanasius—the famous defender of Trinitarian orthodoxy—almost assuredly did not write it.[39] It appeared well after Athanasius died. Here "Athanasian" doesn't mean Athanasius wrote it, but that it reflects his Trinitarian theology.

As you read this creed in full, please notice the great detail with which it explains the nature of Trinitarian unity, the incarnation, and its simple claim of orthodox eschatology.

The Athanasian Creed

Whoever wishes to be saved must, above all else, hold the true Christian[40] faith. Whoever does not keep it whole and undefiled will without doubt perish for eternity.

This is the true Christian faith:

> That we worship one God in three persons and three
> persons in one God without confusing the persons
> or dividing the divine substance.

> For the Father is one person, the Son is another, and
> the Holy Spirit is still another, but there is one
> Godhead of the Father and of the Son and of the
> Holy Spirit, equal in glory and coequal in majesty.

> What the Father is, that is the Son and that is the Holy
> Spirit:

> > the Father is uncreated,
> > the Son is uncreated,
> > the Holy Spirit is uncreated;
> > the Father is unlimited,
> > the Son is unlimited,
> > the Holy Spirit is unlimited;
> > the Father is eternal,
> > the Son is eternal,
> > the Holy Spirit is eternal;

> > > and yet they are not three eternals but one
> > > eternal,

just as there are not three who are uncreated
and who are unlimited, but there is one who
is uncreated and unlimited.
Likewise the Father is almighty,
the Son is almighty,
the Holy Spirit is almighty,
and yet there are not three who are
almighty
but there is one who is almighty.
So the Father is God,
the Son is God,
the Holy Spirit is God,
and yet they are not three gods but one God.
So the Father is Lord,
the Son is Lord,
the Holy Spirit is Lord,
and yet they are not three lords but one
Lord.
For just as we are compelled by Christian truth to
acknowledge each person by himself to be God and
Lord, so we are forbidden by the Christian religion
to say that there are three Gods or three Lords.
The Father was neither made nor created nor
begotten by anybody.
The Son was not made or created but was
begotten by the Father.

The Holy Spirit was not made or created or
begotten but proceeds from the Father
and the Son.

Accordingly there is one Father and not three
Fathers,

one Son and not three Sons,

one Holy Spirit and not three Holy Spirits.

And among these three persons none is
before or after another, none is greater
or less than another, but all three persons
are coequal and coeternal, and accordingly, as has been stated above, three persons are to be worshiped in one Godhead,
and one God is to be worshiped in three
persons.

Whoever wishes to be saved must think thus about the
Trinity.

It is also necessary for eternal salvation that one
faithfully believe that our Lord Jesus Christ became
man, for this is the right faith:

That we believe and confess that our Lord
Jesus Christ, the Son of God, is at once
God and man:

he is God, begotten before the ages of the
substance of the Father,

and he is man, born in the world of the
substance of his mother,

perfect God and perfect man, with
reasonable soul and human flesh,
equal to the Father with respect to his
Godhead and inferior to the Father with
respect to his manhood.

Although he is God and man, he is not two
Christs, but one Christ: one, that is to say,
not by changing the Godhead into flesh
but by taking on the humanity into God,
one, indeed, not by confusion of substance but by unity in one person.

For just as the reasonable soul and the flesh
are one man, so God and man are one
Christ, who suffered for our salvation,
descended to the dead,[41] rose from the
dead, ascended into heaven, is seated
on the right hand of the Father, whence
he shall come to judge the living and the
dead. At his coming all men shall rise
with their bodies and give an account of
their own deeds. Those who have done
good will enter eternal life, and those
who have done evil will go into everlasting fire.

This is the true Christian faith. Unless a man believe this firmly
and faithfully, he cannot be saved.[42]

PSALM 68:32-33

O kingdoms of the earth, sing to God;
      sing praises to the Lord, Selah
to him who rides in the
      heavens, the ancient heavens;
      behold, he sends out his
            voice, his mighty voice.

ENDNOTES

1. Teresa Wantanabe, "The Year of Believing in Prophecies," *Los Angeles Times*, March 31, 1999. Accessible online at articles.latimes.com/1999/mar/31/news/mn-22793.

2. Robert Culver has noted the relatively modern use of this terminology: " 'Eschatology' has an interesting sound. After theology students hear the word they like to use it. It rolls off the tongue easily. It is a modern word invented by theologians which apparently wasn't even in our language until about 160 years ago. It is a fortuitous choice, created no doubt by some scholars who noticed that the word *eschatos* occurs about fifty times in the New Testament for such finalities as the resurrection of the dead (John 6:39, 40, 44, 54; 11:24), the judgment of the 'last day' (John 12:48), and the 'last day' of history (John 11:24, 28) as well as 'last days' or 'times' of the present age (2 Tim. 3:1; James 5:3; 1 Peter 1:5, 20; 2 Peter 3:3)." Robert Duncan Culver, *Systematic Theology: Biblical and Historical* (Ross-shire, UK: Mentor, 2005), 1008.

3. Donald Bloesch has bluntly stated: "Eschatology, perhaps more than any other branch of theology, is laden with divisiveness, and this is particularly true in conservative evangelical circles." Donald G. Bloesch, *The Last Things: Resurrection, Judgment, Glory* (Downers Grove, IL: InterVarsity Press, 2004), 28.

4. Donald Fairbairn observes: "If one looks at patristic eschatology as a whole, it becomes apparent that there are relatively few references to what we today call millennial questions. The

early church placed enormous stress on the return of Christ, the bodily resurrection of believers and unbelievers, the last judgment, and the eternal condition, but in comparison with these emphases, patristic writers expended much less effort to describe the relation between the return of Christ and the thousand-year kingdom of Revelation 20." See Donald Fairbairn, "Contemporary Millennial/Tribulational Debates: Whose Side Was the Early Church On?," in *A Case for Historic Premillennialism: An Alternative to "Left Behind" Eschatology*, eds. Craig L. Blomberg and Sung Wook Chung (Grand Rapids: Baker Academic, 2009), 107. Patristic studies addresses the lives, teaching, and writings of Christians in the first few centuries of church history.

5. Russell Moore, "Personal and Cosmic Eschatology," in *A Theology for the Church*, ed. Daniel L. Akin (Nashville: B&H Academic, 2007), 859.

6. Gerald Bray, *God Is Love* (Wheaton, IL: Crossway, 2012), 723. See also Herman Bavinck, *Reformed Dogmatics: Holy Spirit, Church, and New Creation*, 4 vols., trans. John Vriend, ed. John Bolt (Grand Rapids: Baker Academic, 2003-2008), 4:692.

7. I am greatly indebted to The Bible Project's animations and charts on this subject. I have borrowed much from them while adapting the content to my own nuanced perspective. The Bible Project has an excellent video explanation of this theme in Scripture: www.youtube.com/watch?v=Zy2AQlK6C5k.

8. See T. Desmond Alexander, *From Eden to the New Jerusalem: Exploring God's Plan for Life on Earth* (Grand Rapids: Kregel Academic, 2009).

I've drawn together the content of these charts from a variety of sources: G. K. Beale, *The Temple of God and Church's Mission: A Biblical Theology of the Dwelling Place of God* (Downers Grove, IL: IVP Academic, 2004); G. K. Beale and Mitchell Kim, *God Dwells Among Us: Expanding Eden to the Ends of the Earth* (Downers Grove, IL: InterVarsity Press, 2014); and T. Desmond Alexander, *From*

Eden to the New Jerusalem: Exploring God's Plan for Life on Earth (Nottingham, UK: InterVarsity Books, 2008).

9.   In his discussion of the events of the consummation, John Frame writes that we often place our focus on the wrong aspect of the consummation: "The chief event is, of course, the return of Christ, his second coming. In this discussion, theologians have often focused on the relation of Jesus' return to the *millennium*, the thousand-year period mentioned in Revelation 20. In my judgment, this is somewhat unfortunate. Scripture mentions the millennium specifically only in Revelation 20. And when it speaks about the return of Christ, it is more interested in the impact of that hope upon our lives today than on the scheduling of the events." John M. Frame, *Salvation Belongs to the Lord: An Introduction to Systematic Theology* (Phillipsburg, NJ: P&R Publishing, 2006), 300–301.

10.   Randy Alcorn's book *Heaven* provides a much-needed theology of heaven that explores these topics as well as other frequently asked questions about the nature of eternity.

11.   Michael Bird has rightly observed: "There is a deeply practical side here, for how we act in the present is deeply impacted by what we think of the future. What we think about evangelism, justice, ecological responsibility, pastoral care, budgets, the church, and ethics is based on what God has done and yet will do for his people through Jesus Christ. If our actions echo into eternity, if we contribute something to God's coming kingdom, we will be constrained to operate with a kingdom perspective." *Evangelical Theology* (Grand Rapids: Zondervan, 2013), 236.

12.   One of my favorite quotes regarding our future hope comes from Russell Moore when he writes: "A Christian's eschatology does not consist of his prophecy charts but in his funeral service." Russell Moore, "Personal and Cosmic Eschatology," in *A Theology for the Church*, 858.

13. "In my view, when Scripture tells us about the return of Christ, it doesn't give us this information so that we can put it on a chart and watch the events pass by. That would be catering to our intellectual pride, among other things. Why, then, does Scripture have so much to say about the last days? So that we can reorder our lives in the light of Jesus' coming." John M. Frame, *Salvation Belongs to the Lord*, 311.

14. For an extended explanation of Revelation 20, see Grant R. Osborne, *Revelation: Verse by Verse*, Osborne New Testament Commentaries (Bellingham, WA: Lexham Press, 2016), 321–36; N. T. Wright, *Revelation for Everyone* (Louisville, KY: Westminster John Knox, 2011), 175–86.

15   Some of the material in the sections next four sections has been adapted from the helpful chart "Views of the Millennium" in the *Faithlife Study Bible* (Rev 21).

16. For an excellent cross-examination of these key passages, see Darrell Bock, ed., *Three Views on the Millennium and Beyond* (Grand Rapids: Zondervan, 1999).

17. I only highlight the broad details of agreement in what is historically understood as postmillennialism in the chapter discussion. For more on the points of agreement and disagreement within postmillennialism, check out Kenneth Gentry's essay in *Three Views on the Millennium and Beyond*.

18. There are subcategories to each of these divisions as well. One of the notable (and growing) subsystems is what is called progressive dispensationalism.

19. For a more detailed treatment of eschatology throughout church history, see Gregg Allison, *Historical Theology: An Introduction in Christian Doctrine* (Grand Rapids: Zondervan, 2011), 683–701.

20. Eusebius, *Ecclesiastical History* 3.39.11–12.

21. Eusebius, *Ecclesiastical History* 3.39.12.

22. Justin, *Dialogue with Trypho* 80.4.

23. Nailing down doctrinal specifics among early Christian writings (outside of the New Testament) is quite difficult—not because early Christians didn't define their theological terms clearly, but because we've experienced 2,000 years of linguistic and conceptual refinement. Early Christians aren't beholden to our terms and framing of doctrinal questions. Sometimes our questions would be foreign to past generations of the church; for example, see Joel Beeke and Mark Jones, *A Puritan Theology* (Grand Rapids: Reformation Heritage Books, 2012), 774. Because of this some scholars identify Augustine as amillennial, others as proto-postmillennial.

William Shedd (1820–1894)—a premillennialist—gives an accurate and intellectually honest summary: "[Premillennialism's] most flourishing period was between 150 and 250. Its prevalence in the church at that time has been much exaggerated. That it could not have been the catholic and received doctrine is proved by the fact that it forms no part of the Apostles' Creed, which belongs to this period, and hence by implication is rejected by it. In the preceding period of the apostolic fathers, 100 to 150, it had scarcely any currency. There are no traces of it in Clement of Rome, Ignatius, and Polycarp. In Barnabas, Hermas, and Papias it is found; but these are much less influential names than the former. The early apologists Tatian, Athenagoras, and Theophilus do not advocate it. Alford (on Rev 20:4–5) is greatly in error in saying that 'the whole church for three hundred years from the apostles understood the two resurrections in the literal premillenarian sense.' " See William Greenough Thayer Shedd, *Dogmatic Theology*, ed. Alan W. Gomes, 3rd ed. (Phillipsburg, NJ: P&R Publishing, 2003), 863–64. Louis Berkhof (1873–1957) makes a similar comment about the absence of premillennialism in many early church writings: "There is no trace of it in Clement of Rome, Ignatius, Polycarp, Tatian, Athenagoras, Theophilus, Clement of Alexandria, Origen, Dionysius, and other important

Church Fathers." See Louis Berkhof, *The History of Christian Doctrines* (Carlisle, PA: Banner of Truth, 2002), 262.

24. This theme remains in contemporary dispensationalism: America somehow represents hope in a world soon to be plunged into universe-shaking horrors.

25. Some of these themes are explored in Edwards's *A History of the Work of Redemption*, which wasn't published until 1774. It's available online via edwards.yale.edu.

26. Nathan O. Hatch, "The Origins of Civil Millennialism in America," in *Reckoning with the Past*, ed. D. G. Hart (Grand Rapids: Baker Books, 1995), 87.

27. Crawford Gribben, *Writing the Rapture* (Oxford: Oxford University Press, 2009).

28. Ronald E. Heine, *Classical Christian Doctrine: Introducing the Essentials of the Ancient Faith* (Grand Rapids: Baker Academic, 2013), 177.

29. Still, amillennialism, premillennialism, and postmillennialism can claim antiquity. As Baptist theologian Millard Erickson says, "Although all three millennial positions have been held virtually throughout church history, at different times one or another has dominated." See Erickson, *Christian Theology*, 3rd ed. (Grand Rapids: Baker, 2013), 1107.

30. See Dayton Hartman, *Church History for Modern Ministry: Why Our Past Matters for Everything We Do* (Bellingham, WA: Lexham Press, 2016), 14.

31. Hartman, *Church History for Modern Ministry*, 16.

32. Ben Myers, *The Apostles' Creed: A Guide to the Ancient Catechism*, Christian Essentials (Bellingham, WA: Lexham Press, 2018), 2.

33. Myers, *The Apostles' Creed*, 3–5.

34. On baptism in the Nicene Creed, see Hartman, *Church History for Modern Ministry*, 71–72.

35. For more on these creeds, see Hartman, *Church History for Modern Ministry*, 71–73.

36. "There is no question at all but that the history of this whole matter has been rather sad because there has been dogmatism where dogmatism is not justified at all. People have exaggerated their theories, turning them into facts, and have even made such views the test of people's orthodoxy. When this happens, then I think it becomes very serious. There are, for example, three possible views with regard to the millennium. You can be a premillennialist, a post-millennialist or a non-millennialist (amillennial) and you will find equally saintly people—as I shall show you—belonging to the three groups. ... To elaborate theories and to make them tests of orthodoxy is surely to wrest the Scriptures—as Peter puts it—to your own destruction (2 Pet 3:16). Where we cannot be certain, we must be careful. We must be guarded in our speech and in our language and we must always try to define the point beyond which we cannot go with certainty." David Martyn Lloyd-Jones, *The Church and the Last Things* (Wheaton, IL: Crossway Books, 1998), 87.

37. Athanasius, *On the Incarnation* 27, trans. John Behr, Popular Patristics Series 44b (Yonkers, NY: St. Vladimir's Seminary Press, 2011), 78.

38. *Book of Common Prayer* (New York: Church Publishing Incorporated, 1979), 363.

39. I heartily recommend Athanasius's *On the Incarnation*.

40. Tappert renders "catholic" as "Christian" throughout this translation. Catholic in this sense means the universal church, not specifically the Roman Catholic Church. See Theodore F. Tappert, ed., *The Book of Concord* (Philadelphia: Fortress Press, 1959).

41. Appears in the creed as "hell." See Hartman, *Church History for Modern Ministry*, 70–71.

42. Theodore F. Tappert, ed., *The Book of Concord* (Philadelphia: Fortress Press, 1959), 19–21.

BIBLIOGRAPHY

Alcorn, Randy. *Heaven*. Carol Stream, IL: Tyndale House Publishers, 2004.

Alexander, T. Desmond. *From Eden to the New Jerusalem*. Grand Rapids: Kregel Academic, 2009.

Allison, Gregg. *Historical Theology: An Introduction in Christian Doctrine*. Grand Rapids: Zondervan, 2011.

Athanasius. *On the Incarnation*. Translated by John Behr. Popular Patristics Series 44b. Yonkers, NY: St. Vladimir's Seminary Press, 2011.

Bavinck, Herman. *Reformed Dogmatics*. 4 vols. Translated by John Vriend. Edited by John Bolt. Grand Rapids: Baker Academic, 2003–2008.

Beale, G. K. *The Temple of God and Church's Mission: A Biblical Theology of the Dwelling Place of God*. Downers Grove, IL: IVP Academic, 2004.

Beale, G. K., and Mitchell Kim. *God Dwells Among Us: Expanding Eden to the Ends of the Earth*. Downers Grove, IL: InterVarsity Press, 2014.

Beeke, Joel, and Mark Jones. *A Puritan Theology*. Grand Rapids: Reformation Heritage Books, 2012.

Berkhof, Louis. *The History of Christian Doctrines*. Carlisle, PA: Banner of Truth Trust, 2002.

Bird, Michael. *Evangelical Theology*. Grand Rapids: Zondervan, 2013.

Bloesch, Donald G. *The Last Things: Resurrection, Judgment, Glory*. Downers Grove, IL: InterVarsity Press, 2004.

Bock, Darrell, ed. *Three Views on the Millennium and Beyond*. Grand Rapids: Zondervan, 1999.

Book of Common Prayer. New York: Church Publishing Incorporated, 1979.

Bray, Gerald. *God Is Love*. Wheaton, IL: Crossway, 2012.

Culver, Robert Duncan. *Systematic Theology: Biblical and Historical*. Ross-shire, UK: Mentor, 2005.

Erickson, Millard. *Christian Theology*. 3rd ed. Grand Rapids: Baker, 2013.

Eusebius, *Ecclesiastical History*. Translated by Pail Maier. Grand Rapids: Kregel Academic, 2007.

Fairbairn, Donald. "Contemporary Millennial/Tribulational Debates: Whose Side Was the Early Church On?" In *A Case for Historic Premillennialism: An Alternative to "Left Behind" Eschatology*, edited by Craig L. Blomberg and Sung Wook Chung, 105–31. Grand Rapids: Baker Academic, 2009.

Frame, John M. *Salvation Belongs to the Lord: An Introduction to Systematic Theology*. Phillipsburg, NJ: P&R Publishing, 2006.

Gribben, Crawford. *Writing the Rapture*. Oxford: Oxford University Press, 2009.

Hartman, Dayton. *Church History for Modern Ministry: Why Our Past Matters for Everything We Do*. Bellingham, WA: Lexham Press, 2016.

Hatch, Nathan O. "The Origins of Civil Millennialism in America." In *Reckoning with the Past*, edited by D. G. Hart. Grand Rapids: Baker Books, 1995.

Heine, Ronald E. *Classical Christian Doctrine: Introducing the Essentials of the Ancient Faith*. Grand Rapids: Baker Academic, 2013.

Justin. *Dialogue of Justin with Trypho, a Jew*. In *The Apostolic Fathers with Justin Martyr and Irenaeus*, edited by Alexander Roberts, James Donaldson, and A. Cleveland Coxe. Buffalo, NY: Christian Literature Company, 1885.

Lloyd-Jones, David Martyn. *The Church and the Last Things*. Wheaton, IL: Crossway Books, 1998.

Moore, Russell. "Personal and Cosmic Eschatology." In *A Theology for the Church*, edited by Daniel Akin, 858–59. Nashville: B&H Academic, 2007.

Myers, Ben. *The Apostles' Creed: A Guide to the Ancient Catechism*. Christian Essentials. Bellingham, WA: Lexham Press, 2018.

Osborne, Grant R. *Revelation: Verse by Verse*. Osborne New Testament Commentaries. Bellingham, WA: Lexham Press, 2016.

Shedd, William Greenough Thayer. *Dogmatic Theology*. Edited by Alan W. Gomes, 3rd ed. Phillipsburg, NJ: P&R Publishing, 2003.

Wantanabe, Teresa. "The Year of Believing in Prophecies," *Los Angeles Times*, March 31, 1999. Accessible online at articles.latimes.com/1999/mar/31/news/mn-22793.

Wright, N. T. *Revelation for Everyone*. Louisville, KY: Westminster John Knox, 2011.